THE WILD WORLD OF ANIMALS

POLAR BEARS

MARY HOFF

CREATIVE EDUCATION

Special thanks to Dr. Nick Lunn, research scientist, Canadian Wildlife Service.

Published by Creative Education, 123 South Broad Street, Mankato, Minnesota 56001. Creative Education is an imprint of The Creative Company. Designed by Rita Marshall. Production design by The Design Lab. Photographs by Corbis (Academy of Natural Sciences of Philadelphia, Theo Allofs, Tom Brakefield, Bruce Burkhardt, John Conrad, W. Perry Conway, Dan Guravich, Rob Howard, Wolfgang Kaehler, Sergei Karpukhin/Reuters, Galen Rowell, Sea World of California, Scott T. Smith, Joseph Sohm; Visions of America, Hans Strand, Brian A. Vikander, Kennan Ward, Randy Wells), kevinschafer.com. Copyright © 2006 Creative Education. International copyright reserved in all countries. No part of this book may be reproduced in any form without written permission from the publisher. Printed in the United States of America. Library of Congress Cataloging-in-Publication Data: Hoff, Mary King. Polar bears / by Mary Hoff. p. cm. — (The wild world of animals). ISBN 1-58341-353-7. 1. Polar bear—Juvenile literature. I. Title. II. Wild world of animals (Creative Education). QL737.C27H63 2004. 599.786—dc22. 2004056247. First edition 9 8 7 6 5 4 3 2 1

It's spring in the **Arctic**. Everything is still white with snow and ice. But the air is warm, and the sun is shining brightly on the awakening land. Suddenly, a chunk of snow flies into the air. A black nose sticks out from a hole in the ground. A mother polar bear claws her way to the surface from her den, shaking snow from her thick coat. She looks behind her as another black nose emerges. Soon, two cubs come tumbling out to meet her, blinking at the brightness of the first daylight they have ever seen.

Polar bears live in a land of wind and snow **5**

BEAR OF THE SEA

Polar bears are the largest of all bears. Male polar bears can weigh more than 1,500 pounds (680 kg). Females are about half that size. When standing on its hind feet, a large polar bear can reach 10 feet (3 m) into the air!

Except for the tip of its nose, a polar bear's body is covered with fur. The fur usually looks white, but sometimes oil from the polar bear's food stains it and makes it look off-white or yellowish. Underneath its thick coat, a polar bear has black skin.

Polar bears live in the Arctic on sea ice.

Other animals that live in the Arctic include

caribou, arctic foxes, muskoxen, and snowy

owls. Polar bears are **predators**. Their

favorite food is the ringed seal, but they

will also eat other kinds of seals. Sometimes

they eat walruses and whales, too.

8   An Arctic fox (above) and a harp seal pup (opposite)

The polar bear's scientific name, *Ursus maritimus*, means "bear of the sea." Polar bears are good swimmers. They paddle with their front feet and steer with their back feet. They can swim up to six miles (9.7 km) per hour. One bear once swam more than 60 miles (97 km) without stopping! When swimming, a polar bear can stay underwater for more than a minute.

Life surrounded by snow, ice, and cold air has many challenges. Polar bears have several **adaptations** that make it possible for them to survive in the far northern part of our planet.

Polar bears keep their eyes open underwater   **11**

Some adaptations help them stay warm. Their thick fur and a layer of fat under their skin **insulate** them from the cold air and water. A polar bear can have up to two inches (5 cm) of fur on top of four inches (10 cm) of fat.

Other adaptations help polar bears move from one place to another and catch food. The rough bottoms of their paws give them a good grip on the slippery ice, while their sharp, curved claws help them climb on it.

Strong claws help polar bears climb steep cliffs **13**

The claws also come in handy for capturing their **prey**. Bears' sharp teeth help them grab and hold on to seals. Their whitish fur provides **camouflage** and helps them sneak up on other animals without being seen against a background of ice and snow.

Polar bears blend in with their white surroundings

LIFE AS A POLAR BEAR

Polar bears are hunters. They often hunt for seals by sitting next to an opening in the ice. A patient bear waits for hours for seals to come up for air. When a seal appears, the bear grabs it with its long, strong claws or with its teeth. Seal hunting is easier in the spring and summer than in the winter. Baby seals leave the snow dens in which they were born, and adult seals come out of the water to **molt**, providing the bears with plentiful food.

Polar bears catch and eat a seal every four or five days

Although hunting is easier in the spring and summer, these seasons bring challenges, too. Polar bears' thick fur and fat make it easy for them to become overheated. The ice sheets begin to melt, and some bears are forced to live on land for a while.

Polar bears mate in the spring. In October or November, most pregnant female polar bears dig dens into the deep snowdrifts or, in some places, the earth. They curl up inside as the opening of

18   A three-month-old polar bear cub peers at its reflection

the den fills with snow. The bear doesn't **hibernate**, but her **metabolism** slows, so she doesn't use as much energy as usual.

The mother bear gives birth in the den, usually to two cubs, in December or January. The newborns are about 1 foot (30 cm) long and weigh 1.3 to 1.7 pounds (590–770 g). They spend several months in the den with their mother, drinking the milk she produces and staying warm with the help of her body heat.

Mother polar bears are very protective of their cubs **19**

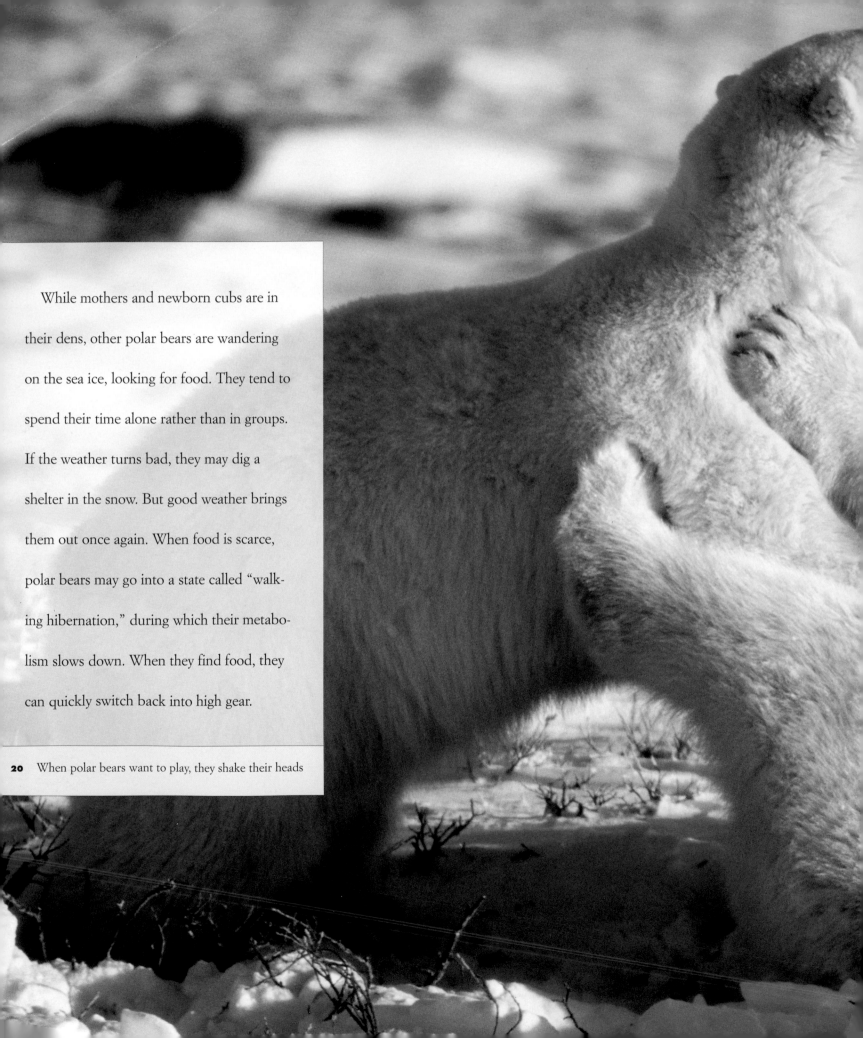

While mothers and newborn cubs are in their dens, other polar bears are wandering on the sea ice, looking for food. They tend to spend their time alone rather than in groups. If the weather turns bad, they may dig a shelter in the snow. But good weather brings them out once again. When food is scarce, polar bears may go into a state called "walking hibernation," during which their metabolism slows down. When they find food, they can quickly switch back into high gear.

When polar bears want to play, they shake their heads

Mother bears and cubs come out of their dens in March or April. The mother teaches the cubs to hunt. The cubs build their muscles and develop their skills by wrestling with each other. Polar bear cubs stay with their mothers for two to three years. Less than half survive their first year. Many cubs starve to death. A polar bear that survives to adulthood commonly lives more than 20 years.

Young bears don't hurt each other when they wrestle **21**

POLAR BEARS AND PEOPLE

Since ancient times, polar bears have been

important to humans. Three thousand

years ago, natives of Greenland, a large

island between northern Europe and North

America, carved images of polar bears from

A man uses a special tool to carve a piece of ivory

ivory. Polar bears also have a place in legends and stories told by native people of the North. Some tales tell about creatures that are both polar bear and human. Many people believed polar bears had spirits that would help them in times of need. Some hunters would speak to the spirit of a polar bear after they killed it to thank it for the gift of meat and fur.

Some ancient people built stone traps to capture bears **23**

The Inuit, native people of the far northern part of the world, called polar bears
nanook. They hunted polar bears with dogs
and with weapons called harpoons, which
are sharp like an arrow but are thrown
rather than shot from a bow. The Inuit
used the polar bears' meat for food, fur for
clothing, and other parts for medicine.

24   The Inuit still dogsled through polar bear territory

Later, polar bears became important to people as a source of recreation. Nonnative hunters traveled to the Arctic to hunt polar bears for sport. Over the years, the number of polar bears killed by humans increased. People began to worry that polar bears might become **extinct**. In 1973, Norway, Denmark, the United States, Canada, and the USSR (now Russia) signed an agreement to protect polar bears.

Members of a hunting party stand over their kill, 1891 **25**

Today, there are about 22,000 to 25,000 polar bears in the world. Many tourists travel thousands of miles to see polar bears in the wild. Hunting is controlled by laws. In Russia and Norway, people may not hunt polar bears. The United States, Greenland, and Canada allow only some polar bear hunting.

"Tundra buggies" keep tourists safe from curious polar bears **27**

Because of the laws, hunting today is not endangering polar bears. However, polar bears face other dangers from humans. Some people think pollution made by humans is harming polar bears' health. **Global climate change** could destroy polar bear habitat by causing the sea ice to melt.

Polar bears spend as much time on ice as on land

Will polar bears survive and thrive in the future? That depends on people, because people are having more and more of an impact on the Arctic. But if we understand polar bears' needs and meet them, these large Arctic creatures will remain a healthy part of our wild world.

In the summer, polar bears live in 24-hour sunlight   **31**

GLOSSARY

Adaptations are things about a plant or animal that help it survive where it lives.

The **Arctic** is the part of Earth that is near the North Pole.

Camouflage is coloring that helps make an animal hard to see in its surroundings.

An animal that is **extinct** can no longer be found alive anywhere on Earth.

Global climate change is a worldwide change in weather patterns caused in part by human activities such as burning gas and oil.

When animals **hibernate**, their breathing and heartbeat slow down, and they use much less energy than usual.

When things **insulate** an animal, they help protect the animal from heat or cold.

Ivory is a hard, white substance that makes up the tusks of animals such as walruses and elephants.

Metabolism is the process by which a living thing converts food to energy for living.

To **molt** is to shed old fur or feathers in order to make room for new fur or feathers.

Predators are animals that kill and eat other animals.

The animals an animal eats are its **prey**.

BOOKS

Biel, Timothy. *Polar Bears*. Poway, Calif.: Wildlife Education, 1997.

Hemstock, Anni. *The Polar Bear*. Mankato, Minn.: Capstone Press, 1999.

Patent, Dorothy Hinshaw. *Great Ice Bear: The Polar Bear and the Eskimo*. New York: Morrow Junior Books, 1999.

WEB SITES

Enchanted Learning http://www.EnchantedLearning.com/subjects/mammals/bear/Polarbearcoloring.shtml

Kids' Planet: Polar Bear http://www.kidsplanet.org/factsheets/polar_bear.html

National Geographic.com Kids http://www.nationalgeographic.com/kids/creature_feature/0004/polar.html

INDEX